PHYSICAL SCIENCE

COLOR
AND
SHAPE

by Mary Lindeen

NORWOOD HOUSE PRESS

DEAR CAREGIVER, The *Beginning to Read—Read and Discover Science* books provide young readers the opportunity to learn about scientific concepts while simultaneously building early reading skills. Each title corresponds to three of the key domains within the Next Generation Science Standards (NGSS): physical sciences, life sciences, and earth and space sciences.

The NGSS include standards that are comprised of three dimensions: Cross-cutting Concepts, Science and Engineering Practices, and Disciplinary Core Ideas. The texts within the *Read and Discover Science* series focus primarily upon the Disciplinary Core Ideas and Cross-cutting Concepts—helping readers view their world through a scientific lens. They pique a young reader's curiosity and encourage them to inquire and explore. The Connecting Concepts section at the back of each book offers resources to continue that exploration. The reinforcement activities at the back of the book support Science and Engineering Practices—to understand how scientists investigate phenomena in that world.

These easy-to-read informational texts make the scientific concepts accessible to young readers and prompt them to consider the role of science in their world. On one hand, these titles can develop background knowledge for exploring new topics. Alternately, they can be used to investigate, explain, and expand the findings of one's own inquiry. As you read with your child, encourage her or him to "observe"—taking notice of the images and information to formulate both questions and responses about what, how, and why something is happening.

Above all, the most important part of the reading experience is to have fun and enjoy it!

Sincerely,

Shannon Cannon

Shannon Cannon, Ph.D.
Literacy Consultant

Norwood House Press • P.O. Box 316598 • Chicago, Illinois 60631
For more information about Norwood House Press please visit our website at
www.norwoodhousepress.com or call 866-565-2900.
© 2018 Norwood House Press. Beginning-to-Read™ is a trademark of Norwood House Press.
All rights reserved. No part of this book may be reproduced or utilized in any form or by any
means without written permission from the publisher.

Editor: Judy Kentor Schmauss

Designer: Lindaanne Donohoe

Photo Credits:

Shutterstock, cover, 1, 3, 6-7, 8-9, 10-11, 11 (inset), 12-13, 14-15, 18-19, 20-21, 22-23, 26-27; iStock Photo, 4-5, 16-17, 24-25

Library of Congress Cataloging-in-Publication Data

Names: Lindeen, Mary, author.
Title: Color and shape / by Mary Lindeen.
Description: Chicago, IL : Norwood House Press, [2017] I Series: A beginning
  to read book I Audience: K to grade 3.
Identifiers: LCCN 2017002620 (print) I LCCN 2017015573 (ebook) I ISBN
  9781684041145 (eBook) I ISBN 9781599538822 (library edition : alk. paper=
Subjects: LCSH: Matter-Properties-Juvenile literature. I Color-Juvenile
  literature. I Physics-Juvenile literature.
Classification: LCC QC173.36 (ebook) I LCC QC173.36 .L56 2017 (print) I DDC
  530.4–dc23
LC record available at https://lccn.loc.gov/2017002620

Library ISBN: 978-1-59953-882-2   Paperback ISBN: 978-1-68404-101-5

302N—072017
Manufactured in the United States of America in North Mankato, Minnesota.

cloth

paper

Everything you can see
is made of something.

This book is made of paper.

These shirts are made of cloth.

3

Paper and cloth are materials.

Wood is a material, too.

wood

plastic

Plastic is another kind
of material.

Materials have their own special features called properties.

Metal is a material that's hard and smooth.

Hard and smooth are properties of metal.

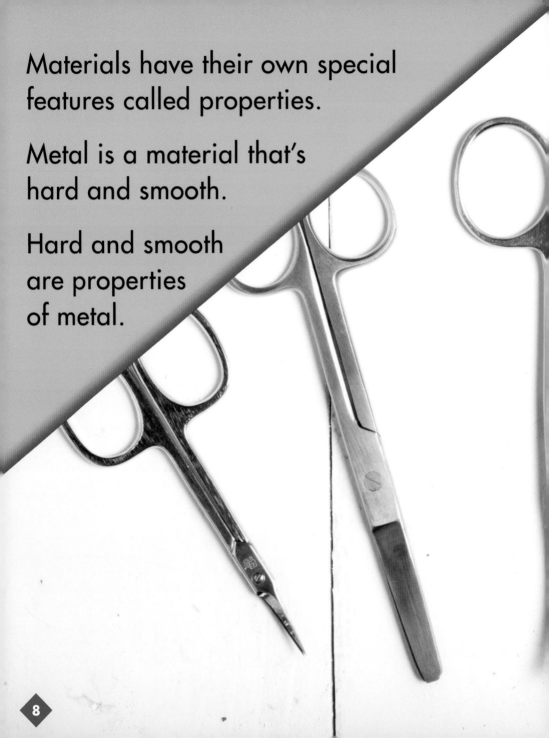

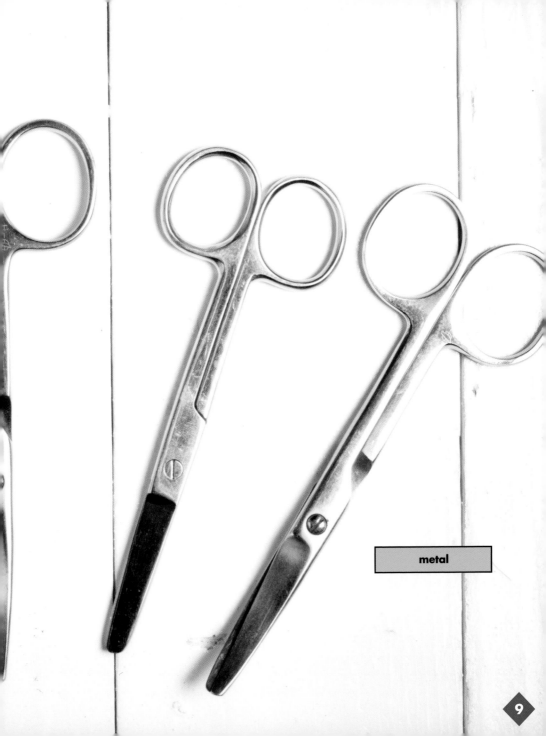

metal

Rubber is a material that's soft and light.

Soft and light are properties of rubber.

rubber

Did You Know?

The most popular color in the world is blue.

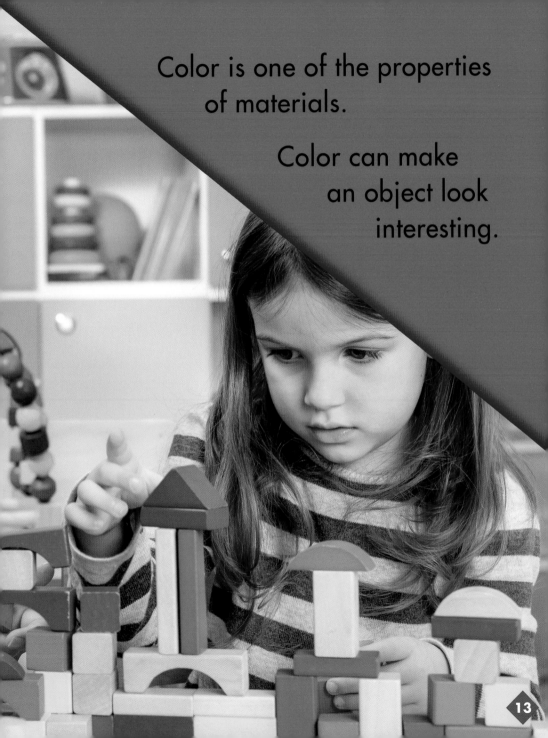

Color is one of the properties of materials.

Color can make an object look interesting.

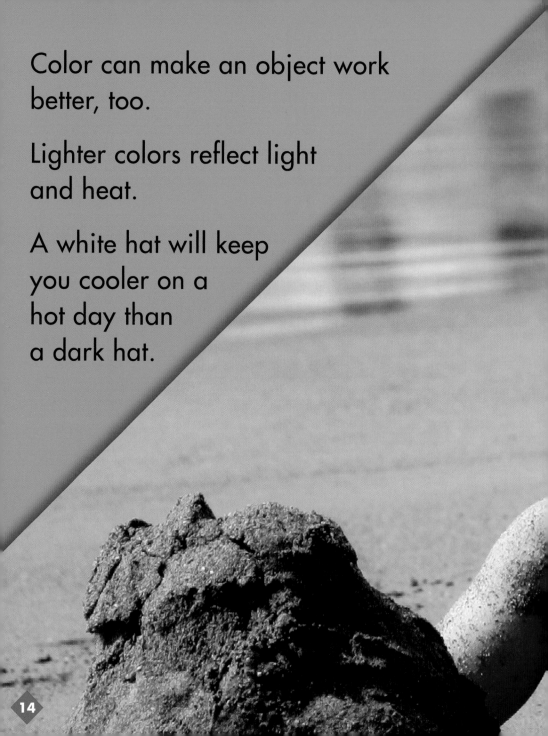

Color can make an object work better, too.

Lighter colors reflect light and heat.

A white hat will keep you cooler on a hot day than a dark hat.

Color can make it easier
to see an object.

Color can also make it harder to see an object.

Shape is another property
of materials.

It is easy to change
the shape of
some materials.

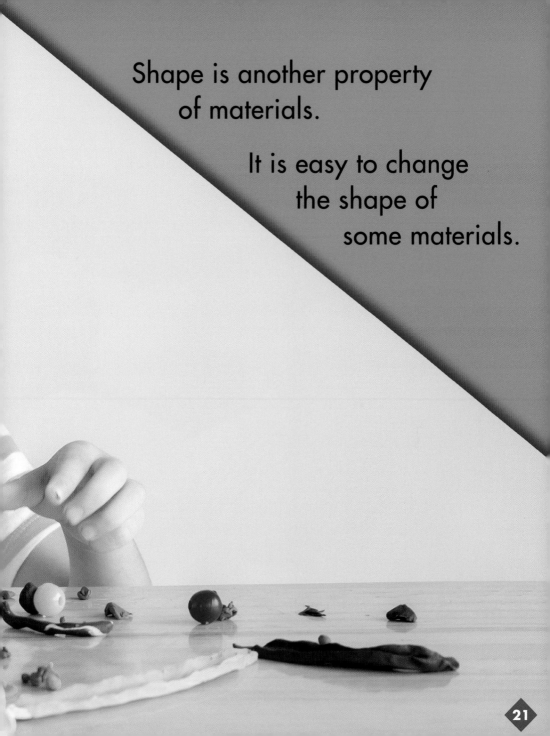

It's hard to change
the shape of others.

Sometimes you want materials
that can change their
shape easily.

Sometimes you want materials
that will not change shape!

Take a look at the things around you.

What materials, colors,
and shapes do you see?

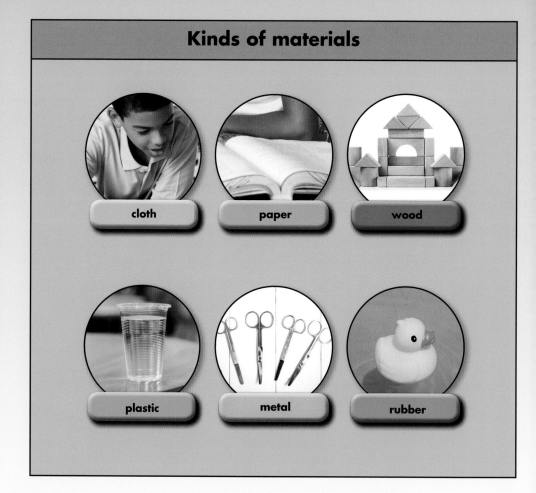

Kinds of materials

cloth

paper

wood

plastic

metal

rubber

Properties of materials

. . . Color . . .

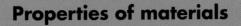

| looks interesting | reflects heat | easy to see | hard to see |

. . . Shape . . .

| easy to change | hard to change | easy to change | hard to change |

CONNECTING CONCEPTS

UNDERSTANDING SCIENCE CONCEPTS

To check your child's understanding of the information in this book, recreate the following graphic organizer on a sheet of paper. Help your child complete the organizer by identifying the main idea of this book and four supporting details.

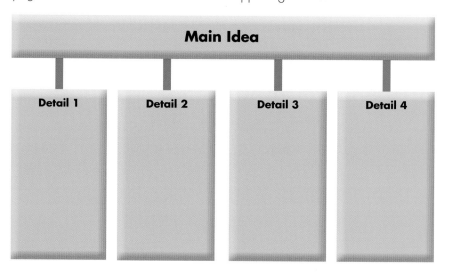

Main Idea

Detail 1   Detail 2   Detail 3   Detail 4

SCIENCE IN THE REAL WORLD

With your child, take a walk around your house, inside and out. Notice the objects you see. Talk about the materials the objects are made of. Talk about the color of the objects. Then talk about the shape of the objects.

SCIENCE AND ACADEMIC LANGUAGE

Make sure your child understands the meaning of the following words:

materials   metal   features   properties   liquids   object   popular

Have him or her use the words in a sentence.

FLUENCY

Help your child practice fluency by using one or more of the following activities:

1. Reread the book to your child at least two times while he or she uses a finger to track each word as it is read.

2. Read a line of the book, then reread it as your child reads along with you.

3. Ask your child to go back through the book and read the words he or she knows.

4. Have your child practice reading the book several times to improve accuracy, rate, and expression.

FOR FURTHER INFORMATION

Books:

Hansen, Amy. *Matter Comes in All Shapes.* Vero Beach, FL: Rourke, 2011.

Kalman, Bobbie. *What Is It Made From?* New York, NY: Crabtree, 2011.

Mason, Helen. *Is it Hard or Soft?* New York, NY: Crabtree, 2014.

Websites:

Bitesize: Materials

http://www.bbc.co.uk/bitesize/ks2/science/materials/material_properties/read/1/

PBS Learning Media: Finding the Strongest Shape

http://tpt.pbslearningmedia.org/resource/phy03.sci.phys.mfe.zcolumnsi/columns-finding-the-strongest-shape/

Physical Science: Grouping Materials

http://www.bbc.co.uk/schools/scienceclips/ages/6_7/grouping_materials.shtml

Word List

Color and Shape uses the 93 words listed below. *High-frequency* words are those words that are used most often in the English language. They are sometimes referred to as sight words because children need to learn to recognize them automatically when they read. *Content words* are any words specific to a particular topic. Regular practice reading these words will enhance your child's ability to read with greater fluency and comprehension.

High-Frequency Words

a	blue	is	one	the	what
also	both	it	other(s)	their	white
an	called	look	own	these	will
and	can	made	see	things	work
another	day	make	some	this	world
are	do	most	something	those	you
around	from	not	take	to	
at	have	of	than	too	
be	in	on	that	want	

Content Words

better	dark	hat	light(er)	plastic	smooth
book	easier	heat	liquids	popular	soft
change	easily	hot	material(s)	property(ies)	sometimes
chocolate	easy	interesting	metal	reflect	special
cloth	everything	it's	milk	rubber	syrup
color(s)	features	keep	object	shape(s)	that's
cooler	hard(er)	kind(s)	paper	shirts	wood

About the Author

Mary Lindeen is a writer, editor, parent, and former elementary school teacher. She has written more than 100 books for children and edited many more. She specializes in early literacy instruction and books for young readers, especially nonfiction.

About the Advisor

Dr. Shannon Cannon is an elementary school teacher in Sacramento, California. She has served as a teacher educator in the School of Education at UC Davis, where she also earned her Ph.D. in Language, Literacy, and Culture. As a member of the clinical faculty, she supervised pre-service teachers and taught elementary methods courses in reading, effective teaching, and teacher action research.